Tree
Island

Sue Arengo

Oxford University Press

The Norman family were on a ship called The Princess Diana. Denis Norman and his wife, Brenda, were with their two children, Martin and Marina.

'Good morning, everyone!' said the captain. 'The island you can see over there is called Fruit Tree Island. If you want to visit it, please go down into the boat.'

'Come on, Denis,' said Mrs Norman.

'You can swim or go for a walk,' said the captain, 'but please come back here before three o'clock. We must be on the ship at three o'clock.'

'Let's go for a walk,' said Martin. 'It's not too hot. We can take some nice photographs with Dad's camera.'

The Normans went up a hill in the centre of the island.
'I can see all of the island from here!' said Martin.
'Oh, yes,' said Mrs Norman. 'And look! There's our ship!'
'What's the time, Dad?'
Mr Norman looked at his new watch. 'Two o'clock. We need
to leave now.'
When the Normans arrived at the beach, nobody was there.
'Where is everybody?' cried Mrs Norman. 'Where's the
captain? Where's the boat?'
'Perhaps this is the wrong beach,' said Martin.
Then Marina saw something. 'Oh, no!' she said. 'Look!'
Far away they could see The Princess Diana – leaving the
land!

• Why was nobody at the beach when the Normans
arrived?

'Your watch must be wrong, Dad,' said Marina.

'It can't be,' said Mr Norman. 'It's new. I got it on the ship yesterday.'

'Let me see it,' said Martin. 'Oh Dad! It's a *Tock* watch! They always go wrong. Everyone knows that.'

'I didn't know,' said Mr Norman.

'You know now,' said his wife. 'Oh Denis! What are we going to do? We can't stay here!'

'It's all right, Brenda,' he said. 'Lots of ships come here.'

'But where are we going to sleep?' she said. 'And what are we going to eat?'

'It's all right, Mum,' said Martin. 'Tomorrow we can make a shelter. And there are lots of things to eat: there are fish in the sea, and fruit on the trees.'

He started to make a map of the island. 'Look! I'm making a map to help us.'

Martin showed his map to the family.
'Tomorrow we can make a shelter,' he said.
'Tonight we can sleep here, under these trees,' said Marina.
'Sleep?' cried Mrs Norman. 'I don't think I can sleep tonight!'

• Match the names on Martin's map to the places you can see on page 4. Where is the best place to make their shelter? Remember: they need to be near the sea (for fish, and to see ships), a river (for water), and trees (to make their house).

In the morning, Martin and Marina looked at the map again.

'Green Tree Circle looks nice,' said Martin. 'There are lots of trees there and it's near a river, too.'

'Yes, but the beach is too small,' said Marina. 'I think the best place for our shelter is Half Circle Beach. There are some trees, there's a river and it's next to the sea. And it's near Long Beach so we can easily see if a ship arrives.'

The Normans began walking to Half Circle Beach. They saw lots of different fruit trees. Marina got lots of fruit from the trees.

'Look in your book, Martin,' she said. 'And tell me if we can eat these fruits.'

Island fruits

Some island fruits are dangerous!

1 A water melon is dark green. It is red inside and has lots of very small black stones. This fruit is wonderful if you are thirsty.

2 A pineapple is large and yellow-brown. It is good if you are thirsty or hungry.

3 A coconut is brown with brown hairs. The fruit is white and there is some sweet water called coconut milk.

4 A redberry is a little red fruit with orange leaves. The redberry trees are beautiful, but the fruit can make you ill.

5 A banana is long and green or yellow. It is good if you are hungry.

6 An avocado is small and dark green. The fruit is yellow-white and is good to eat.

7 A blue sun fruit is round and yellow with lots of little blue hairs. Do not eat this fruit: it can kill you.

8 A mango is green and orange. The fruit is orange and very good to eat.

• Name the fruits you can see in the picture on page 6.

At last they arrived at Half Circle Beach. Martin got some fish from the sea. Mr Norman made a fire.

Mrs Norman sat under two big leaves and put her hands behind her head. 'I didn't like that ship much,' she said. 'There were too many people on it and they made too much noise.'

'I liked it,' said Marina. 'The discos were really good.'

It was very hot and very quiet on the beach. The only noise came from the sea.

'How are we going to make the shelter?' asked Mrs Norman.

'There are some pictures in this book,' said Martin.

'Are we going to have hot water?' asked Marina. 'I want to wash my hair!'

'You can wash your hair in the river,' her brother laughed. 'We're going to make a shelter, not a hotel!'

Here are six different shelters you can make.

1. THE ROCK SHELTER

2. THE WOOD SHELTER

3. THE TALL SHELTER

4. THE LITTLE HOUSE SHELTER

5. THE LEAF SHELTER

6. THE ROUND HAT SHELTER

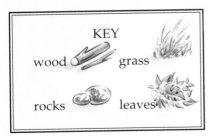

KEY

wood grass

rocks leaves

- Which shelter can the Normans make?

They could only make one shelter.

'The Wood Shelter looks nice,' said Marina. 'Let's make that one.'

'We can't,' said Martin. 'There are only twenty little trees there and the Wood Shelter needs more than that. We can only make the Little House Shelter.'

Before the Normans could make the shelter, they needed some wood, leaves and grass.

Mr Norman cut down some trees.

'You're doing well, Denis!' said his wife. She liked to see her husband working hard.

'Here you are, Mum!' called Marina. 'Here are more big leaves!'

When they had everything they needed, Martin and Marina started to make the shelter.

In the evening, they sat and talked about their home in England.

'We had a nice house, didn't we?' Mrs Norman said. She took some photographs from her bag. 'Here's a picture of us all.'

'Oh yes,' Marina said. 'That was last Christmas. That's my red dress. And look! Here we are in the garden!'

• Look at the photographs of the house in England. Now look at the shelter. Write down three things that are different about the outside, and three things that are different about the inside.

The Normans finished the shelter. Now they didn't have anything to do.

Martin sat on a rock, and looked out to sea. 'Let's go for a swim,' he said. 'The water's beautiful. Come on, Marina!'

Martin and Marina swam far away from the beach. Then, suddenly, they saw something strange.

'Look!' cried Marina. 'A boat!'

It was an old boat, made of wood. She arrived first, and got onto it.

'Hello! Is anybody there?' she called, but there was no answer. 'Come on! Let's see if anybody is inside.'

'Be careful!' said Martin.

There was nobody on the boat – but they saw some photographs of the captain.

'He must be dead,' said Marina.

'No,' said Martin. 'I think he's on the island.'

'Why?' she asked.

He didn't answer. 'When we go back, let's walk,' he said. 'Then we can take a few things to the shelter.'

• Why does Martin think the captain is alive and on the island? (Look at page 10 again.)
Find five things that Martin and Marina can take. What can they carry the things in?

'I think the captain swam to the island,' Martin said, 'because I saw some things at Half Circle Beach. I think I saw a hat – the hat he's wearing in those photos.'

They walked back and Martin found the captain's old hat under the trees.

'You see, I'm right!'

'But is he alive now?' said Marina.

'I don't know.' Martin put on the captain's hat. 'Let's go and look for him tomorrow.'

Back at the shelter, they told their mother and father about the old boat.

'Look!' said Marina. 'Two knives! Now we can cut that pineapple! And we've got some coffee and two bottles of lemonade!'

In the morning, Martin and Marina went to look for the captain. They saw the old boat again, and then they walked for a long time, away from the sea.

Martin didn't have his map, but Marina had a map from the boat.

'Where are we?' she asked.

They looked at the map.

'Oh no!' they cried. 'All the places have different names.'

• Where are they? Where is Half Circle Beach?

Marina looked at the map and found Half Circle Beach.
'Here it's called "Little East Beach",' she said. 'And that hill must be North Hill. On this map it's called "Old Rock Hill".'
'OK,' said Martin. 'Now let's go this way.'

They came to a river. The water was fast and dangerous.
'It's too dangerous,' said Marina. 'We can't swim across that.'
'But we can't go back now,' said Martin.
'Well, I'm not swimming!' Marina answered.
They looked up and down the river. They needed to find something to help them cross it.
'I'm hungry!' said Marina. 'I'm thirsty and I'm tired. I want to go back to the shelter. We can't cross this river.'
'Yes, we can,' said Martin. 'But we need to think carefully.'

• How can Martin and Marina cross the river?

Marina found the answer. 'I know!' she said. 'We need that long piece of wood! We walk to the end of the bridge. Then we can get across to the rock.'

Across the river there were a lot of tall, dark trees. Behind the trees, they saw a beautiful garden and . . . a big, strong shelter.

'Hello!' they said loudly. 'HELLO!'

They saw the captain, and told him their story. He was very friendly.

'So it was because you had a *Tock* watch!' he laughed. 'I must remember never to buy one!'

'Yes,' they said sadly. 'And now we want to go home. We're waiting for a ship.'

'Come and have a drink,' he said. 'You must be thirsty.' He took them to his shelter. There were two beautiful little trees near the door.

'What are these?' asked Martin. 'They're not in my book.'

'Island Life trees.' The captain smiled. 'I grew them.'

In the shelter, they drank from wood cups. There was some Island Life fruit on the table.

'Can I eat one?' asked Martin.

'Of course!' said the captain. 'But be careful . . . it's a strange fruit.'

'Is it dangerous?' asked Marina

'No,' he smiled. 'It just makes you feel a bit different.' He watched them eat.

'So, you want to go back to England, do you?' he said.

'No, we don't,' said Martin.

'No.' Suddenly Marina laughed. 'We want to stay here.'

• Why is the fruit strange?

Mr and Mrs Norman arrived in the garden.

'We came to find you!' said Mr Norman.

They met the captain and asked him a lot of questions.

'How often do ships come here?'

'About four times a year,' he said.

'Why are you here, then? Why don't you leave?' they asked.

The captain smiled. 'Because I like it here. I don't want to leave.'

'Here you are, Mum and Dad,' said Martin. 'Have some Island Life fruit.'

One day, about two years later, two young tourists visited the island, and went for a long walk. They met the Normans.

'You look very happy here,' said the young man.

'We are!' The Normans smiled.

Soon it was time for the young tourists to leave. Marina watched them go. 'I think we are going to see them again very soon. Very, very soon,' she said.

'Oh?' said her family. 'Why do you think that?'

But Marina didn't answer. She only smiled.

• Why does Marina think they are going to see the young tourists again very soon?

Glossary

beach place beside the sea

boat a small ship

bridge a way for people to cross a river

captain most important person on a ship

fire when you burn wood to cook things, or be warm

fish animal that lives in the sea

fruit something you can eat, like bananas and apples

grow (past **grew**) when plants and trees get bigger and taller

inside in

island land with water all around it

leaf (pl. **leaves**) green parts on a tree

map plan of a place that shows where you are

outside out

piece part of something

rock a big stone

shelter place where you are safe from the sun, rain and cold

snake a long animal with no legs

swim (v) move your body in the water

tourist someone on holiday

way (n) how you go from one place to another

wood it comes from trees; you can make a house from it

Answers to the puzzles

page 3
Because Mr Norman's watch was wrong and they arrived too late. (See picture on page 2.)

page 9
Number 4: the Little House Shelter

page 11
The shelter is smaller, it is made of wood, there is no garden, it only has one window, etc.
The shelter only has one room, there is no bathroom, no stairs, no pictures on the stairs, no television, etc.

page 13
They can take: two knives, some coffee, two pairs of trousers, two shirts, a map, two bottles of lemonade. They can put it in the big wooden box.
Martin saw the captain's hat under some trees on Half Circle Beach, so he thinks he might be alive.

page 15
They are in Flower Circle (called Million Flower Place on Martin's map). Half Circle Beach is called Little East Beach on this map.

page 17
They can put the long piece of wood from the bridge to the rock, and from there they can jump to the other side.

page 19
Because when Martin and Marina eat it, they don't want to go back to England. They want to stay on the island!

page 21
Because the young woman had a *Tock* watch.

page 5
Half Circle Beach is the best place for the shelter.

page 7

Oxford University Press, Great Clarendon Street, Oxford OX2 6DP

Oxford   New York
Athens   Auckland   Bangkok   Bogota   Bombay
Buenos Aires   Calcutta   Cape Town   Dar es Salaam
Delhi   Florence   Hong Kong   Istanbul   Karachi
Kuala Lumpur   Madras   Madrid   Melbourne
Mexico City   Nairobi   Paris   Singapore
Taipei   Tokyo   Toronto

and associated companies in
Berlin   Ibadan

OXFORD and OXFORD ENGLISH are trade marks
of Oxford University Press

ISBN 0 19 422482 1

© Oxford University Press 1993

First published 1993
Sixth impression 1996

No unauthorized photocopying

Cover illustration by Gary Wing

Illustrated by Gary Wing

Typeset by Wyvern Typesetting Ltd, Bristol

Printed in Hong Kong